Our voice in our future

**Shaping Our Lives: project workers –
Michael Turner, Phil Brough and R.B. Williams-Findlay**

JR
JOSEPH
ROWNTREE
FOUNDATION

The **Joseph Rowntree Foundation** has supported this project as part of its programme of research and innovative development projects, which it hopes will be of value to policy makers, practitioners and service users. The facts presented and views expressed in this report are, however, those of the authors and not necessarily those of the Foundation.

Joseph Rowntree Foundation
The Homestead, 40 Water End, York YO30 6WP
Website: www.jrf.org.uk

Shaping
Our Lives

Shaping Our Lives is a national research and development project run by service users. It is working to establish a national network of organisations controlled by service users including: disabled people, older people, people with learning difficulties and users and survivors of mental health services. Shaping Our Lives are also working to make links with a wide range of other service users.

ISBN 1 85935 117 4   (paperback)
ISBN 1 85935 118 2   (pdf: available at www.jrf.org.uk)

A CIP catalogue record for this report is available from the British Library.

Cover design by Adkins Design

Prepared and printed by:
York Publishing Services Ltd
64 Hallfield Road
Layerthorpe
York
YO31 7ZQ
Tel: 01904 430033   Fax: 01904 430868   Website: www.yps-publishing.co.uk

Further copies of this report, or any other JRF publication, can be obtained either from the JRF website (www.jrf.org.uk/bookshop/) or from our distributor, York Publishing Services Ltd, at the above address.

CONTENTS

Acknowledgements

Thanks are particularly due to the people involved with the local projects:

- Phil Brough, the worker for Shropshire Disability Consortium's part in the project, and to Sue Bott, the Consortium's manager.

- Everyone on the Steering Group for the work that took place in Sheffield: Christine Barton and John Mitchell (Sheffield Centre for Inclusive Living), Jason Chadburn, Michael Coston and Tina Willamson (Speaking up for Action), Alden Chadwick and Rachel Jackson (Sheffield City Council), Jacquie Stubbs (Sheffield Forum of Disabled People) and Jasmine Warwick (Voluntary Action Sheffield).

- Bob Williams-Findlay, the consultant to the Sheffield project.

- Margaret Hogan, ex-communications manager at the now defunct National Institute for Social Work, for input on the three Our Voice in Our Future (OVIOF) booklets.

POSTSCRIPT

Since this report was drafted, the Joseph Rowntree Foundation (JRF) has revised its programmes and priorities. The Future of Rights and Welfare programme has not proceeded as originally planned. However a new programme – Independent Living – is scheduled to start in late 2003, and it is intended to feed the results of the Shaping Our Lives projects into this new programme.

Alex O'Neil, JRF Research Manager

INTRODUCTION

Our Voice in Our Future (OVIOF) was established by the Shaping Our Lives (SOL) project in 1999 in response to a request from the Joseph Rowntree Foundation (JRF) to facilitate user involvement in a new funding programme, initially called Shaping Futures and subsequently changed to the Future of Human Rights and Welfare.

The programme sets out to involve service users in the debate on the future of welfare, rights and entitlement in social care and disability. OVIOF was set up to start this process by identifying the key issues for service users.

Before starting the project, Shaping Our Lives ran an initial project to involve a range of service users defining the project. This process is described in Chapter 2 of this report.

This has been a long and sometimes difficult project, taking substantially longer than originally anticipated. However, the difficulties experienced – which have been largely associated with the low resourcing and capacity of local user-controlled organisations – are as much a part of the findings as the results of the work that did take place.

PART I

PROJECT OVERVIEW AND WORK AT NATIONAL LEVEL

1 DESIGNING AND ESTABLISHING THE PROJECT

Before starting the project, Shaping Our Lives was keen to engage a wide range of service users in shaping the project. To achieve this, an initial project was carried out which involved:

- a survey of the 300 user groups on the Shaping Our Lives database to get their views and experiences of good and bad practice in user involvement

- a review of good and bad practice as recorded in current literature on user involvement

- a seminar with representatives of user organisations to discuss general principles of user involvement and specific details about the shape and structure of a project.

The three strands of the preparatory project produced a firm set of indicators of what service users see as the key principles that should underpin user involvement and consultation, which were used in the development of the full project.

Respondents to the survey reported generally poor experiences of involvement, with a view from many respondents that the process was tokenistic and had little real impact on the decision-making process.

Good experiences of user involvement were characterised by strong and ongoing relationships between users and service providers backed up with financial resources for independent, user-controlled organisations. This reflects the key findings of most of the literature on the issue.

The seminar was a key part of the design process. It involved a range of service users including:

- people with physical impairments
- people with sensory impairments
- the deaf community
- older people
- mental health service users/survivors
- people with learning difficulties
- people living with HIV/AIDS
- young people in care
- users from ethnic communities.

Notes of the seminar are reproduced in the Appendix. It addressed some general issues around user involvement before moving on to specific discussions around the shape and structure of the proposed project.

Participants at the seminar put the case for a project that used the expertise of existing user organisations, addressed policy and practice issues, put an emphasis on collating and networking its findings, and used its findings both for the JRF's programme and for wider political lobbying on the issues raised.

A large-scale national project backed up with local work carried out by user-controlled organisations was developed in the seminar. It was recognised that this was an ideal model of the project that would have required an unrealistic amount of funding.

Subsequent work addressed how the ideal model could be moulded into something achievable within the funding available. Three outline proposals were developed based on the plans that had been developed in the seminar. Participants were then consulted about which proposal they wanted to be expanded and put to the JRF for funding.

The result was a project that would work intensely in two locations to promote and facilitate discussion of the long-term future of welfare by service users and user-led organisations, backed up by work at a national level.

This included the use of questionnaires and a set of three booklets to ensue that these discussions were fully informed about developments and debates on the future on welfare.

As well as being fed into the JRF's programme, the proposal included work to ensure that the conclusions were disseminated around user groups and as widely as possible, with a particular emphasis on ensuring that they reached politicians and the media.

2 NATIONAL WORK: BOOKLETS AND QUESTIONNAIRES

A set of three booklets were produced covering key issues in social policy: benefits, services and support, and mental health issues for the project's national work. The last subject had been particularly identified by the Shaping Our Lives National User Group as being of particular importance because of the review of the mental health legislation that began at about the same time as this project.

The booklets were designed with two purposes. They were intended to examine developments in social policy relating to issues that they covered and to stimulate discussion of those issues. They were written in an accessible format, with easy-access summaries, and they included at the back a questionnaire, which readers were encouraged to fill in and return to Shaping Our Lives.

Debatable issues were particularly highlighted by the booklets. These issues included:

- levels of benefits
- the emphasis on benefit fraud
- charges for social care services
- support for mental health service users and survivors
- the emphasis on public safety in mental health policies.

The booklets were distributed widely and were well received. Around 300 were distributed directly to user-controlled organisations on the Shaping Our Lives database.

Other copies were sent out on request in response to publicity for the project and reviews of the booklets themselves in the following quantities:

- benefits: 326
- services and support: 411
- mental health issues: 512.

Systems for recording the number of copies that were sent out were not perfect and there is likely to have been a degree of under-recording. For example, members of the Shaping Our Lives National User Group took bulk numbers to distribute in their areas but the quantities have not been recorded.

The number of copies of the mental health issues booklet distributed and the fact that mental health service users/survivors were the largest single group of people to respond to the booklets and questionnaire, indicates that the National User Group was correct to identify this as a key issue for the project to address.

The response rate to the questionnaires in the booklets was actually very poor. With hindsight, the format of putting the questionnaire within the booklet was not the best way to obtain a response – it did not make it easy in terms of having a form that could just be filled in and returned. The people who did respond did so by letter.

When Shaping Our Lives did a follow-up mailing to the groups on its database, there was a better response but, with just 26 responses in total, this part of the project has to be seen as having failed.

It is probably also true to say that not enough follow-up work was carried out. Shaping Our Lives' resources and staffing were limited during the period in which the project ran. Another issue may have been that its public profile was not strong enough to generate what had been planned as a major national debate. Shaping Our Lives has since grown from being a project to an organisation.

Having said all this, if success is judged on the quality of the responses rather than the quantity, the national survey was a great success.

Results of the questionnaires

Value of the welfare state

Most respondents recognised that the value of the welfare state went beyond that for the individual user and their families/supporters, pointing out the wider benefit to society as a whole. One person made the point: 'Extreme poverty is not compatible with democracy' and another suggested that 'care in the community is the mark of a civilised society'.

People also spoke about the welfare state in terms of it giving an equal right to services and support. There was a suggestion that the welfare state should 'give the opportunities to take a full part in society' and that it should embrace education, employment, housing and transport, as well as health and social care, and benefits.

It was also suggested that, in the future, the welfare state should become less paternalistic and address issues around exclusion. One person suggested that the welfare state should be available 'not as a safety net but as a bridge to enable those people who are marginalised to integrate into society in every way'.

Another point was made that the beneficiaries of the welfare state include 'the vast army of service professionals who prescribe people's needs, apply the social controls and manage the segregated provisions made for excluded people whether they need protecting/managing or not'.

This respondent also said that the welfare state fails to benefit the people whom it is meant to serve but 'the only satisfactory outcome is full inclusion'.

A similar observation was made about commercial companies benefiting from the welfare state, in particular the drug companies.

Benefits

Levels of payment

Some respondents said that benefit levels are reasonable but most believed that they are too low, with one person highlighting the growing gap between wages and benefits.

One respondent made the point that 'flat-rate levels do not take account of the range of circumstances and factors such as housing costs, transport accessibility, local authority provision and charges and strength of voluntary pension', and suggested that a more localised benefits system would address people's needs more effectively.

An older person pointed to the difficulties faced by people with small private pensions that brought them just above income support levels, therefore denying them associated benefits such as council tax benefits and free glasses.

In its response, the Derbyshire Centre for Inclusive Living said that it is important to look at benefits giving 'the same sense of confidence and control ... as earned income'. It suggested that the purpose of benefits needs to move from compensating to enabling, saying that there are signs that this is starting with the introduction of tax credits.

Fraud

There was clear support for fraud to be tackled:

> Fraud is a crime and should be prosecuted in any form.
> (Derbyshire Centre for Inclusive Living)

However, almost everyone who addressed this issue believed that the approach to benefit fraud needs to be more realistic and that the issue is currently over-played. One respondent said:

> Targeting of specific groups of genuine probable offenders would be far fairer than the present branding of recipients. The onus on reporting or informing on claimants by the public is deplorable and inequitable and denies the state's responsibility in this. Identifying the reasons for fraud to its real cause would be conducive to tackling its root causes.

There was also a suggestion that, with a realistic approach and better use of the technology that is now available, fraud could be tackled more effectively than it is at present.

The point was made that checks on many benefits have revealed little in the way of fraud. Two people suggested that the emphasis on fraud is a deliberate move by the government to distract attention from the low levels of many benefits.

One respondent believed that the media is having too great an influence:

> Letting policy be dictated by the gibbering of the more rabid tabloids has been a disgraceful dereliction of duty by policy makers for many years.
> (Derbyshire Centre for Inclusive Living)

Another respondent called for there to be an equal emphasis on the take-up of benefits.

One respondent appeared to be trying to explain some of the fraud that takes place, saying that:

> The law says it's fraud. Those of us who have tried to live on basic allowances know how extremely poor the quality of life is at that level. Basic allowances should be increased and only then would it be just to emphasise fraud to those on a basic allowance.

Welfare to work

Welfare to work initiatives were seen as threatening. People thought that there should be a more supportive approach to getting people into work.

Other issues

There was particular criticism of the way that disability benefits are administered through demeaning medical tests and means testing.

Social care services

Respondents generally opposed charges being imposed for care services. Of the few who did agree with charges, one person thought they should be linked to the quality of services and another suggested that they should not be applied to people on benefits.

Opponents called them 'unjustifiable' and a form of double-taxation. One respondent described charges as:

... a sword that has hung over our heads for the last ten years and has haunted all actively involved in user-representative organisations ... Means-tested charging is a nasty policy which singles out disabled people and punishes them for their impairment and dependency.

This is how one respondent put the argument against charging:

Services that 'equalise' citizens should be free to all that need them, i.e. someone should not pay to get out of bed if they need assistance as all people unaffected by disability enjoy this freedom as of right.

Other arguments against charges for services were given a response from Hampshire Centre for Independent Living (HCIL). It described charges as discriminatory and as undermining the human rights of disabled people and contributing to the continuing poverty of many disabled people. Government guidelines stopped councils taking people's earnings into account when assessing charges, but pensions and savings are still taken into account when older people are assessed, and HCIL sees this as a continuing disincentive against disabled people.

Derbyshire Centre for Inclusive Living argued that services cannot deliver appropriate outcomes without proper funding through taxation.

There was support for the view that people should have rights to services. One person specifically pointed out that this should cover all services, not just those relating to 'desperate need'. It was also pointed out that human rights laws now extend to support services.

There seemed to be acceptance of the situation of families continuing to be the main source of social care, though several respondents pointed out the importance of there being adequate support for families and recognition of families' varying circumstances.

One respondent gave the view that people should have at least some choice over this situation and another, Derbyshire Centre for Inclusive Living, pointed out that the key issue is people being able to achieve the outcomes of self-determination and control. To achieve this, people need choice over the source of their support.

Hampshire Centre for Independent Living's discussion of charging policies argued that charges and the assessment procedures for means testing of charges deterred people from asking for services and support.

User involvement

Respondents were very sceptical about current practices around user involvement, with it being characterised as 'patchy and tokenistic' by one person. Another person described there being 'a lot on paper but very little in practice'. This is identical to the finding of the survey that took place in the preparatory project for OVIOF.

Criticisms were made of a lack of commitment to user involvement at a national level. An example was cited of mental health service users/survivors not initially being included on the Expert Committee that reviewed the Mental Health Act and then, when users were recruited to the Committee, they were removed after speaking out against proposals for compulsory community treatment.

Respondents identified the need for strong and well funded local and national organisations if full and proper user involvement was to be achieved. These organisations needed to be 'rooted in grassroots experience' and to be based around setting the purpose and outcomes of services.

People saw it as being important to make user involvement 'exciting and relevant'. Another suggestion was that work in relation to 'quality control' is particularly important for user involvement.

One person pointed to the difficulties of getting mental health service users/survivors involved:

> If someone has a short, sharp attack they probably go back to work and do not have time. The rest of us are either too ill or up to our ears in local representation already.

One respondent raised the need to broaden the range of service users who get involved, making the suggestion that training might help users to get involved. Another suggestion was for there to be a greater emphasis on communication between service providers and service users.

Action is also necessary from service providers to ensure that user involvement becomes more effective. One respondent pointed to the lack of a strategy on user involvement, arguing that it often came down to the individual workers involved in service provision who were prepared to listen to service users:

> Just a few individuals listen to us. Most of the NHS staff cannot hear us.

This person questioned what happens to those who cannot make themselves heard.

Another saw the need for service providers and staff to 'listen and listen again to what the user wants and needs'.

There was also the idea that local authorities should be compelled to hold consultation forums and there was a call for the retention of Community Health Councils.

For survivors, one person pointed to the need for the 'context of an overall service user/survivor belief system or philosophy', which they thought existed but needed to be 'defined and expressed'. Another person said:

We need to tell our stories. They are all different.

The questionnaire asked which was more important – developing user organisations or working with service providers. Developing the user agenda was seen as the priority by some. One person thought:

When we start doing fascinating stuff they'll start looking at us. Trying to influence and change them could get too depressing.

Others pointed to the need to develop credibility through activities like being published in professional journals.

The mental health booklet asked for users'/survivors' views of direct action. Some saw it as a positive step, suggesting that it would also foster solidarity among users. There was concern that direct action could reinforce stereotypes of mental health service users/survivors. Others thought that it 'tends to alienate rather than influence'.

Influencing social care training was also identified as a key activity, with the point made: 'the user's perspective must be a part of educational curricula'.

Several people pointed to the value of the arts as a means of expression. There were also calls for positive images in the media to challenge negative stereotypes.

Respondents supported the idea of different user groups working together:

> Across-the-board dialogue will result in a benefit to society on many issues.

It was suggested that different groups need to identify areas of common interest and start working together on these issues. One person did express concern that different groups working together could fragment what is being achieved but they also saw potential gains in identifying issues that people have in common.

Mental health

The OVIOF project took place at the same time that changes were being proposed to mental health legislation. As mentioned previously, this led to the suggestion of a booklet specifically on mental health issues, which generated the highest level of responses.

These are the key points made on these issues.

- The dominance of the medical model of distress and the resulting emphasis on drug treatments, which many users/survivors disagree with.

- Perceptions of survivors and users among service providers, the public and opinion formers, i.e. politicians and the press, are very negative. Respondents similarly believed that issues around public safety have been exaggerated and that the 'dangers' are no greater now than in the past.

- Having the types of support available that users and survivors are asking for would address and negate the public safety issue. There was a particular call for 'low-level' services that give support before people reach a crisis point and require a more extensive intervention.

- People saw the need for an integrated approach that fully involves the user. Low expectations of users means that they are not seen as able to take any responsibility. People thought that attitudes needed to change for this to be possible.

- Respondents saw employment as important, particularly in terms of giving people a purpose, and sense of belonging was also referred to.

3   ISSUES FROM THE LOCAL PROJECTS

The reports of the projects that took place in Sheffield and Shropshire can be found in Chapters 5 and 6 of this report, and are stand-alone reports of the work that took place in these areas. This chapter looks at some of the issues around setting up the local projects, and the matters of concern that the service users in Sheffield and Shropshire share in common and how these relate to the national survey.

Setting up the local projects proved to be a long and often difficult process. The project proposal recognised that the local work was likely to take place in areas where there were established user organisations and initial approaches to a rural and an urban user organisation were made on this basis. The idea from Shaping Our Lives and the preparatory project seminar was for the projects to be carried out and controlled at the local level, rather than being run and controlled by Shaping Our Lives at a national level.

While the rural project initially set about its work fairly speedily, discussions with an urban group about their taking on the project took some time and the organisation ultimately decided not to undertake the project.

Attempts to find another urban organisation of service users led to initial discussions with two others, which said that they did not have the capacity to take on the work. Advice was sought from the British Council of Disabled People to identify groups that might have the capacity to carry out the work, which resulted in contact with an organisation of disabled people in Sheffield.

Despite initial enthusiasm for the project, there was once again the feeling that the organisation would not have the capacity to take on the work. However, one person from the organisation was keen to look at options for the work to take place in Sheffield and involved the city's Centre for Inclusive Living, which was at that time in its early stages of being established. This led to the establishment of a local steering group that brought together a range of service user interests and the engagement of a consultant to carry out the local project.

This arrangement proved less than perfect and there were a number of problems that are detailed in the report from Sheffield (see Chapter 6). These issues are detailed here to highlight the fact that problems occurred as a result of working with under-resourced user-controlled organisations.

There had been an initial delay to the rural project when external issues caused difficulties in the relationship between Shaping Our Lives and the organisation undertaking the project, along with the worker who had been appointed to the project having to give up work because of health problems.

This led to a mutual agreement to relocate the project and it was then undertaken by the Shropshire Disability Consortium. Subsequently, the rural project went much more smoothly because the work was taken on and controlled at a local level by a well resourced organisation.

Despite these problems, Shaping Our Lives is likely to remain committed in the future to using this approach of working with local service user organisations. User involvement begins at a local level and national projects need to reflect and support this if they are going empower service users and their organisations.

The lesson that Shaping Our Lives and others need to learn from this project is that working in this way takes time. Future projects that follow this model would benefit from a lengthier preparatory project and from giving local organisations more opportunities for input into the main project. This may also foster a greater feeling of ownership of the projects for the organisations set to be involved.

Common issues from the two local projects

Experiences of services

As with other areas of Shaping Our Lives' work, there was a high degree of consistency in users' reports of their experiences of services in Sheffield and Shropshire.

It is a sad indictment of social care services that, whenever service users come together, they share their negative experiences of services. Workers ignoring or not listening to the views of users, home care workers with an inadequate amount of time and social services transport being unreliable or forcing people to leave events when they are not ready were among the complaints made in Sheffield.

Most worrying is the underlying theme that these are not just failings of services but part of the way service providers perceive service users. As the Shropshire report puts it:

> It feels like workers in the social and health care field simply had no respect for service users as equal citizens.

People in Sheffield also focused very much on the impact of poor relationships with the staff who provide services, with comments about staff who complain about their work to service

20

users and are negative about the people that they are meant to be serving.

Participants in both projects were also keen to highlight positive experiences of services. In both Sheffield and Shropshire, they placed great value on supportive staff and an individualised approach to services, and a number of people in Sheffield particularly appreciated access to and support with leisure activities.

The need for a holistic approach to services

Another theme that runs through many of Shaping Our Lives' projects is that service users look at their lives as a whole, not in terms of the structures that services are organised into, and this was again reflected in the projects in Sheffield and Shropshire.

Participants in the Sheffield conference raised concerns about hospital waiting lists, the lack of council housing and inaccessible public transport. They were also particularly concerned to get training and support with finding jobs, with people on benefits also feeling that they were being held back from getting work by the rules about getting benefits.

In Shropshire, people were particularly critical of the way in which services are compartmentalised, which they see as leading to a situation in which different departments are 'precious of their clients'. There was also a general theme around the lack of information, particularly about services and about medical treatments. This was one of the points where the interests of mental health service users/survivors and the parents of disabled children converged, as both were concerned about drugs being prescribed without full explanations of their side-effects.

People in Sheffield wanted to see a 'willingness to try new ways of providing services'. The Shropshire project called for national standards to be established to ensure that all users have access to equal services, with users being involved in drawing up and monitoring the services.

Poor experiences of user involvement

People in Sheffield had had very negative experiences of user involvement.

They made a particular point about the need to ensure that it is service users themselves who are involved, and not just carers and others who represent their needs.

The evident fatigue with consultation in Sheffield was humorously characterised in a sketch about a service user given just a few days to respond to a ten-page questionnaire based on a 60-page document, which she saw as 'too much, too late' before throwing it away.

Despite this, there is still a strong and clear motivation among users to get involved if that involvement is going to lead to real changes and improvements.

Participants in Shropshire made a similar point about there being no point in becoming involved if it was not going to lead to positive results. They called for involvement to start from the very beginning, in setting budgets.

A common approach to user involvement

Both the Sheffield and Shropshire projects were based on the Shaping Our Lives model of involvement working across all different types of service users.

There were some difficulties with how this worked in Sheffield. One of the problems was an unfortunate clash with an event being held by mental health service users and survivors on the same day as the conference, which meant that they were not represented.

One of the successes of the day was the presence of a number of service users who had not previously taken part in user involvement events. This success was qualified by the fact that some of these people were not adequately supported in terms of their communication needs, but this did highlight some important issues that need to be addressed both locally and nationally in terms of developing fully inclusive user involvement.

Another important aspect of the Sheffield project was a successful piece of outreach work with disabled people in the Somali refugee community in the city. This identified a number of common interests with other service users and provided further evidence of the value of a broad-based user movement.

In Shropshire, there were particularly important developments in terms of involving the parents of disabled children as a user group in their own right. Their participation in the project led to the recognition of a number of connections with other groups of service users, including mental health service users/survivors as well as disabled adults.

The report of the Sheffield conference saw the event very much as a starting point of people coming together to speak together, noting:

> People enjoyed working together with different impairment groups and have an interest in pursuing this further.

4   Conclusions

Our Voice in Our Future has been a long and frequently difficult project. Coming at an early point in the development of Shaping Our Lives meant the project lacked the infrastructure and profile to develop a national debate among service users on the future of social policy that had been envisaged at the start of the project. The difficulties with the local projects likewise hampered their work to varying degrees.

The problems with the local work, particularly those that occurred in Sheffield, are in themselves important findings of the project indicating the difficult and fragile state of user involvement at a local level.

Beyond this, the project has produced useful findings, despite the limits to its scope, and some good signposts for issues that the Joseph Rowntree Foundation's programme on the Future of Rights and Welfare is covering, which are highlighted in the recommendations below.

Findings and recommendations

User involvement

User involvement itself emerged as a key issue in both of the local projects and in the questionnaire responses. The project has highlighted the fact that, even with the poor experiences of involvement and consultation, service users still see involvement as the key to improving the quality and outcomes of services.

Many are still prepared to become involved if they can see the prospect of it delivering changes and improvements.

Recommendation: the programme should examine and disseminate good practice on user involvement and engage the government and local authorities in a debate on making user involvement a real and effective force.

Holistic services

The project has again highlighted service users' holistic approach to their lives and the services that they need, and that social care needs to become part of a 'whole systems' approach taking in health care, benefits, transport and support with training and employment.

Recommendation: social and health care services are already beginning to work together much more closely with the advent of primary care trusts. Direct payments can also be seen as delivering a much more holistic approach. The programme should facilitate service users to undertake detailed consideration about the type of support services they want and how existing services could develop in this direction. This could be called 'realistic blue skies thinking', i.e. it should look at ideals that are achievable through measures such as changes in structures and reallocation of resources.

Standards of services

While OVIOF's purpose was to look at the future of social policy, the users who took part inevitably wanted to consider current problems with services that they experience at present. Issues such as the negative attitudes of social care workers to service users emerged again in this project as they have in other areas of work by Shaping Our Lives.

Recommendation: work should be undertaken to assess why basic qualities of service remain absent from a significant proportion of social care and what can be done to remedy the situation. This may be an area of work that could be carried out in conjunction with the General Social Care Council, which is responsible for registration of social care workers and their conduct and practice.

Charges for services

Discussions of social care in this project and elsewhere have focused particularly on charges for home care services. While there have been wide-ranging public discussions of charges for residential care, charges for home care seem to be an invisible issue – although service users clearly see them as a great injustice.

Recommendation: work should be carried out to show evidence of the impact of charges on the lives of service users. There may also be a case for examining the economic validity of charging for home care services and whether they represent an effective means of raising income for local authorities.

Benefits

Respondents to the questionnaire were clearly concerned about the adequacy of benefits and about the current emphasis on people defrauding the benefits system. Participants in the Sheffield conference clearly pointed to being trapped on benefits when they wanted to be able to work.

Recommendation: in recent years, most of the discussion of benefits has been reactive to the government's agenda to the reform of benefits. OVIOF set out with the intention of being proactive and not just responding to existing agendas. Benefits is an area where this could be progressed with discussions about the type of benefits system people would want to see developed, working along the lines of 'realistic blue skies thinking' detailed above.

Mental health

Shaping Our Lives precipitated mental health issues being important to the project by identifying them as a key issue at the start. There was significantly more interest in the booklet on mental health issues than in the other two and the response rate on this issue was higher. The topic was also discussed by participants in the Shropshire project in terms of the prevailing medicalised approach to mental health with users/survivors being treated solely as patients.

Recommendation: work has already been carried out to develop a social model of madness and distress. Further work should be supported in this area and in its promotion and dissemination.

Other issues

A final recommendation is for the programme to particularly look at further work that can specifically take place in the areas where the two OVIOF projects took place, Sheffield and Shropshire. The report from Sheffield clearly points to work that needs to take place in the city to continue the development of user involvement, which would also feed into wider debates on the issue. In Shropshire, participants voiced concerns that the project would raise expectations without supporting further work and, again, there are clear plans to build on the work carried out thus far.

Work on the Future of Rights and Welfare started in mid-2002 with the Joseph Rowntree Foundation funding what is now the

Shaping Our Lives National User Network (SOLNUN) to take on the role of secretariat to the programme. In this role, SOLNUN has established a user-led steering group for the programme which will advise the Foundation about projects to be funded through the programme. This model has already been used effectively by the Joseph Rowntree Foundation in its older people's programme, in which older people have been supported to set the agenda for research in this area.

OVIOF has provided a sound basis for the development of the programme and guidance on issues for the Steering Group to consider for the programme to work on. The learning from the difficulties experienced in the course of the project should also help to ensure that future projects under the programme are developed and carried out more effectively.

On reflection, OVIOF itself has become a preparatory project for the projects that are to come from the Future of Rights and Welfare programme and more widely by SOLNUN, mirroring the preparatory project that took place before OVIOF itself. Viewing OVIOF as part of the development of debates and discussions on the future of social policy, it may achieve the national debate that it set out to hold in the long term.

PART II

LOCAL WORK IN SHROPSHIRE

5   THE SHROPSHIRE REPORT

The Flower of Opportunity model

The Steering Group considered a number of compilation models for the report. The project is about service users and the outcomes that they expect from service providers to improve their quality of life, and a method had to be found to reflect this. It would be easy to classify opinions in the way that services are currently delivered, but that would give credibility to a system that was clearly not working for users. The Egan Plan, which focuses on the 'situation now and hoped for' model, was also considered and attempted, but there was not always a 'now' situation and this would limit the scope for a workable and constructive model. The possibility of using the seven need areas of successful living received support and from that discussion came the idea of using the Living Options Project model created by disabled people in Shropshire. This would give a more realistic approach to the outcomes discussion and place it in a framework that also reflected societal values.

Participants felt it was important to reflect this desire to access the sort of life opportunities in the same way as other people, i.e. to work to potential, to train, to build relationships, to raise families, to access leisure facilities and, most importantly, to receive respect as accepted members of society. This desire, of course, is not reflected in the way that services are delivered and it is clear that a major rethink is necessary by service providers if they are to meet the rising ambitions of service users.

The Living Options Project took place in Shropshire in the early 1990s and was run jointly by the Shropshire Disability Consortium, Shropshire Social Services and the Shropshire Health Authority. Disabled people who participated created a 'flower model' to present the findings. This way of presenting the concerns of the SOL participants is used again, in an attempt to bring order to the findings.

The stamen of the Flower of Opportunity contains three essential elements that are necessary to access other ingredients to live a successful life. These are rights, information and advice. The four petals of the flower are:

- emotional well-being
- physical well-being
- getting around
- living space.

Although an attempt has been made to present this report in a way that will make it both easy to read and easy to refer to, it has proved difficult to achieve a co-ordinated and accessible document that can be used by all interested parties. For example, participants spoke about the negative images presented by the media and the negative way in which society saw them, and presented numerous examples of this, but where in the model would this fit? Should it be under 'emotional well-being' or in any of the other sections? Is it to do with rights and could all service providers presenting a co-ordinated approach address these societal attitudes? Obviously they could, but, since no such co-ordination exists, how could this be presented? Inevitably, some issues will belong to more than one section and some do not seem to fit in anywhere, while others are more easily defined.

The views expressed in this report are those of the project participants; the ideas and the opinions belong to them, the quotations are bullet points only and are a snapshot of discussion, sometimes heated. There was much talk of changing the way in which social services operate, but no conclusion was reached. Questions discussed included the following.

- Should adult services be abandoned and more services managed in the independent sector?

- Should the disabled children's team become part of the children and families social work team, and operate to the same child protection issues?

- Should we have one highly motivated generic family support team?

- Should the health authority provide more community-based services?

- Should we appoint a holistic team, consisting of social services, health, education, housing and employment services in a supportive role?

- Why is there a need for different teams supplying a service to physical, sensory, learning and mental disability users?

Agreement on the answers to the questions was inconclusive, but the participants agreed that the role of social care staff was to empower people to participate fully in mainstream society. Participants believed that current service delivery reinforced the marginalisation that they felt.

This report is written to reflect the format of the meetings. Other points that arose during discussion follow individual service user quotations.

Rights, information, advice

This includes:

- advocacy
- consultation
- information
- joint working
- societal values
- service standards
- training.

People said (in the following comments, SI denotes sensory impaired, DC denotes disabled child and LD denotes learning disabled):

> How many people know about us? Who else has access to our personal information?
>
> (SI service user)

> They gave me medication for my child, but I don't use it. I don't know what the effects are.
>
> (DC parent)

> She [the social worker] said there wasn't any playgroup facilities for her [daughter]. I knew the playgroup's leader who said my daughter could go there. It was a complete lie.
>
> (DC parent)

We just want to be left alone to bring up our child, just the same as anybody else. Why should we spend hours on the phone finding out things? Somebody else could be doing that.

(DC parent)

Why isn't information technology given a higher profile, educating sensory-impaired young people? Is it because the workers haven't got the skills to train them?

(SI service user)

We did some work three or four years ago about deaf/blind people, but we got nowhere.

(SI service user)

We took part in the Social Services Inspectorate's assessment of services and they didn't include anything we said. One of our members was in tears.

(DC parent)

We haven't heard from them [Disabled Children's Register] since we put his name in. Not even a newsletter.

(DC parent)

They put labels on you, I should have 'LD' tattooed on my forehead.

(LD adult)

Every new social worker that we get has to fill in yet another form. Education wants one, the medical people do, it's the same questions all the time. Why can't one form do for all the people that need to know.

(DC parent)

Discussion points

Advocacy

This was something that was discussed at each meeting. The idea that someone who was independent and knowledgeable about the social and health care system could take away the frustrations of dealing with it was an attractive one. Many people felt that an advocacy service would be more useful than a social service. It should be integrated, too, with a team of advocates who could provide support and information on all aspects of service. Advocacy for disabled children has never been addressed. Some parents thought that they were, perhaps, not the best people to speak on behalf of their children. Service providers should not undertake this role either; it needed to be someone independent, perhaps with personal experience of disability.

Consultation

Most participants had heard of some form of consultation and many had taken part but the experience was not positive. It seemed to many people that decisions were made and then users asked to comment, if at all. There were four examples of poor consultation.

- Social services: the various teams organised consultation on budgets, eligibility criteria, etc. But these were always about cuts or reductions in services and users felt that they could never influence decisions at that late stage of the process. It is doubtful that service users would actually agree to cuts in services or reductions in budgets.

- Disabled children's social work team: parents of disabled children were highly critical of the recent consultation exercise carried out by the Shropshire disabled children's social work team. Parents received a questionnaire about cuts in services and were asked which categories of disabled children should be removed from the eligibility criteria. Many parents felt uneasy about deciding those issues and spoke of feelings of guilt in denying another parent a service. All parents felt that a service should be provided if the need was there and, yet, the different agencies could not even agree on how disability was defined, resulting in some families of disabled children not getting a service at all. Parents felt they were taking the responsibility for decisions that were not theirs. If providers could not meet the needs of clients, then that should be recorded as 'unmet need' and ways to meet those needs discussed with service users. If needs could not be met because of a lack of resources, then, once again, partnerships should be forged to look at ways to bring in extra monies. Participants at three meetings talked about a family in Shrewsbury with an autistic child who clearly needed support but this was denied because of the classification of the disability.

- The wheelchair service: the service had run out of money. Did wheelchair users agree to that and what was being done to correct the situation? Did the government department know that needs could not be met?

- Health/social services: participants felt that transition was a new buzzword and that a lot of unnecessary work was being put into a service that was not needed. Disabled and older people and parents of disabled children spoke of the acute lack of even social work teams of the same authority working together. One person said that her notes were not even passed on and she had to have another assessment of need. Teams were very precious of their clients; it felt almost like users belonged to certain teams of professionals and were seen as their property. People thought that the children's and adults' team should work more closely together with education and employment services to produce holistic pathways for disabled children, based on the skills of the child. A dedicated transition team would be just another hurdle to go through. There was no such thing as a transition person and it would mean three teams when one would do.

People said there was little point in becoming involved in consultation if there were no positive results. Service users should be involved in the initial stage, perhaps, when the budgets were being worked out. Users were disempowered, anyway, through the lack of information and by the use of language that professionals understood and took for granted. Some mental health service users were paid user consultants; perhaps this was, indeed, the answer to thorough consultation. Providers needed to realise that they were there to provide a service to people who needed support.

The education authority also received a good deal of criticism from parents of disabled children and from disabled parents. Schools and colleges had little idea of how to meet the needs of disabled parents who wanted to attend parents' evenings and participate in school activities in the same way as other parents. Parents wanted to make informed decisions about the quality of education for their disabled children but faced a wall of indecision. Even fundamental advice about the difference of mainstream or special schools was not forthcoming. Parents could not discover whether equipment was available, or how children with a sensory impairment could access information sources and, worst of all, there was little work done to provide the child with a holistic pathway through the education system and on to work.

Information

This was a major discussion topic at every meeting. People were unable to access the information that they required. Parents could not, for example, find out about holiday grants, or about the current debate on 'special' or 'mainstream' education and their rights to have the education of their choice for their child. Mental health service users were not told about their rights to treatment as members of the community when they left hospital. Older people did not know the duties of carers or how they could complain. Disabled people who used carers had similar problems. One woman had had three different carers in one week and had been given little opportunity to complain. The social service complaints procedure took time and, sometimes, users wanted instant solutions. One mental health service user said that she often wanted support to take her child to school when she felt too ill to do so. It was at times of crisis like this that assistance should be provided – just what were her rights to a service?

Accessible information still appeared to be an issue. Service users found it hard to ask for the information format that they required to participate in everyday life, in the same way that other people could. All information should be available in the necessary format and people given the options. Braille as an alternative written language caused some discussion. If people still used it, then it should be provided; the use of computers with voice input/ output did not suit everyone.

How can service users find out more about who is accountable to whom and how they can influence decisions at a high level? Most participants had not heard of the Scrutiny Panel and that elected councillors had a say in how social and health care services were run. Almost all of the people who took part had heard of the national charities specific to their disability.

All client groups were, consistently, not given information about other statutory services, voluntary groups or contact details of national organisations. Peer support was a vital ingredient in the pursuit of quality of life and it should be policy that all workers know where support groups can be found. This deliberate, as some people thought, withholding of information – presumably to maintain the power advantage – needed to be addressed in policy guidelines. This led to a long debate in Ludlow about the power struggles that exist between the providers and the users. The conclusion reached was that all staff who were involved in the delivery of services should show respect and be trained in equality issues. Disabled people were an oppressed minority in much the same way as black people and women used to be, and needed to be in a position of equality when services were being discussed.

Joint/inter-agency working and service standards

Service users talked about the lack of service cohesion at every meeting. There always seemed to be another assessment form to be completed – why was this necessary? The same information was given to a multitude of people from a variety of agencies. Notes did not even appear to be passed on between social work teams. Participants thought that services should be provided on the terms of the user and not of the provider.

A forceful debate about generic social work took place in a few areas. Some people thought that a highly trained workforce able to support families over long periods of time was the answer. Such a workforce would have a more developmental and advocacy role, and would be able to deal with the extra burdens that society places on service users that prevent them from living fulfilling lives. Parents, in particular, have to wade through a bureaucratic minefield of information and dead ends, and then still do not know what sort of adult life their children will lead. Workers should be able to remove these extra burdens and allow people to concentrate on the mainstream pathways of life, school, training, employment, building relationships, parenting, etc.

Life-skills training supplied by schools, colleges and national charities was ineffective and inappropriate. Colleges are where young people go to enhance skills to prepare them for the workforce, not places to learn how to tie shoelaces. Parents needed to be trained by disabled adults how to teach their disabled children to live with the disability.

Services differed from area to area. National standards should be set and adhered to and users involved in the process. A monitoring system should also be in place. People wanted to know the legislation relating to the frequency of assessments, the use of advocates, their rights, the accountability of workers, local guidelines about the return of phone calls, the complaints procedures, the use of different social workers, rules that carers operated to, etc. When could users expect an answer to queries, a visit from an occupational therapist? Is there a chart of accountability?

Everyone liked the idea of service users running more services but few were aware that the Shropshire Disability Consortium ran services independently of social services.

The greatest criticism of services came from parents of disabled children who faced a mammoth task in untangling the myriad of services that they were forced to access for their children. Social services disabled children's team is usually the first point of contact for parents and yet seemed unable to satisfy their needs. Sometimes it felt that there was a continuous tug-of-war between parents and social workers over the best way forward for their children. Parents' right to parent was often brought into question, with workers feeling that they were, in fact, the experts on the disability. There were complaints of phone calls not being returned, misinformation and dishonesty regarding services that could not be provided. There was reference to intimidation – some of it unintentional, threats of removing existing services and parents felt that social workers had the power to remove disabled children if they believed the children were not progressing to some theoretical standards. There was also an accusation of blatant lying, if not deception, by some workers who, apparently, did not know or would not say what services were available. One parent said that they found out about the direct payments scheme but were threatened with the loss of existing services if they proceeded with the application. Most people did not know how social or health services operated. Who was the manager? Could users complain directly to the manager? What reassurances were possible to ensure that services would not disappear, or that there would be no reprisals. This sense of suspicion about the consequences of complaints or the misuse of personal information existed among all the client groups. One client (mental health service user) felt that she could not trust social services with her care problems because of her fear of having her child taken into care because of her mental health problem.

Some voluntary agencies also came in for their share of criticism. A young visually impaired man had not heard about an active group of visually impaired people that had been in existence since 1989. He was therefore missing out on the experience of talking to other people – people who knew about the systems in place and about visual impairment. Two wheelchair users had had bad experiences with the Wheelchair User Group, who had offered little support with grievances against the wheelchair service. What was the purpose of campaigning groups if they supported the service provider?

Societal values

People had a lot to say about labelling and this topic arose at most meetings. One person said that it felt as if he had 'LD' tattooed on his forehead, and people felt that services were provided to suit the label and disability not the individual. A person born without sight appeared to be expected to live the prescribed life of a blind person and there seemed little opportunity to break away from that expectation. Being seen as an individual in the context of service provision is not an impossibility.

At every meeting, someone spoke about negative comments and discriminatory treatment from members of the public. The public found it hard to accept people who were different, but, if all the agencies operated from the same perspective, this could be addressed. It was a matter of equality-based education and training, and a realisation that disabled people wanted the same things out of life as anyone else and should be given the same opportunities. Service users should be at the forefront of training workers on life issues that affected them.

Training

This was another much discussed topic. It felt as if workers in the social and health care field simply had no respect for service users as equal citizens. Disability was an equality issue in the same way that race and gender issues were years ago. Every worker should undergo disability equality as part of the induction course. The emphasis had to change; workers were employed to provide a service to enhance life chances, not to help people through a bad patch. Participants made direct links to history and scientific experiment, feeling sometimes as if they were part of some great social experiment. Some professionals seemed intrigued by the disability and how it affected functioning in mainstream life.

Emotional well-being

This includes:

- emotional and peer counselling
- mental health
- personal fulfilment
- support.

People said (in the following comments, MH denotes mental health, DC denotes disabled child and SI denotes sensory impaired):

The Monkmoor Day Centre is closing down. What are we going to do now? They promised to ask us what we thought, but the next thing we heard was that it was going to be closed. They didn't turn up for the meeting.

(MH service user)

They [social services] sent us a questionnaire asking us who should get a service and who shouldn't. How could we answer that? We felt so guilty, we didn't fill it in. Everyone who needs a service should get one from somewhere.

(DC parent)

We seem to be part of a massive experiment.

(MH service user)

Services seem to suit the providers, not us.

(Wheelchair user)

I daren't go to social services, although my child is a problem. They know about my problems and if my depression gets worse, they might take my child away.

(MH service user)

All the support the social worker offered was to take my child into foster care. I was so depressed. The health visitor wouldn't tell me anything about my son's disability; she thought I couldn't take it. It was two years before I met another mum who had a disabled child, I thought I was the only one.

(DC parent)

My child belongs to me, not the system.

(DC parent)

We had to wait months just for an assessment.

(DC parent)

They need to realise, they are there to provide us with a service, not the other way around. Sometimes it feels like the services suit the provider, rather than the user.

(Wheelchair user)

Employment services did not seem to do any work in special needs schools. Why don't they try and find jobs that fit the skills of the kids, like they would with normal kids?

(DC parent)

This medical bloke said that he [a mental health service user] was 'not a proper person'.

(MH service user)

> The nearest deaf counsellor is miles away, in Stoke-on-Trent. Counselling services should be using more disabled people to counsel other disabled people.
>
> (SI service user)

Emotional and peer support

Disabled people found difficulty in accessing counselling services; one deaf person said that the nearest deaf counsellor was 40 miles away. It was considered inappropriate for social workers or psychologists to perform this role – people wanted counsellors who had some experience of disability. Peer support was an essential element on the path to empowerment but little information was available at main information points. Most workers seemed reluctant to give this information.

Physical well-being

This includes:

- access
- care
- domestic chores
- medication
- service standards.

People said (in the following comments, DC denotes disabled child, DP denotes disabled parent and MH denotes mental health):

Playtimes are the worst for him. He was allocated a special friend by the teacher but, of course, he wanted to play football with his friends and left. You can't blame his friend, but the school should make more effort so the kids could include him.

(DC parent)

Shared care arrangements are too rigid. Things come up and we want respite care immediately. I would like a block of time to arrange, myself.

(DC parent)

They had to close the Grange Centre early because of snow and sent her [daughter] home and just left her there, on her own. They didn't even let me know.

(DP parent)

They gave me medication for my child, but I don't use it. I don't know what the effects are.

(MH service user)

We do some work for Lucas, I think it is, but we don't get paid. The chargehand is very condescending and the social workers don't understand. We should be paid the same as other workers. They call it training.

(MH service user)

I know that a lot of deaf people are protesting that BSL [British Sign Language] should be a proper language, but they could teach it in schools. Kids would love it, using their hands. The deaf sign-language users wouldn't have a problem later on.

(BSL user)

I think the kids should have exchange visits with other kids from mainstream schools.

(DC parent)

Therapeutic earnings system needs revising. Doing voluntary work should come with a payment and the value of working for a voluntary agency part of the training package to full-time work.

(Various people)

Ritalin is still being prescribed and anti-depressants. I thought there was talk of doing away with that.

(MH service user)

I think there is only one full-time access officer in the county. How can we improve things with that sort of commitment?

(Wheelchair user)

I couldn't attend parents' evenings, I couldn't get in. The LEA [local education authority] were useless, they couldn't understand the issue.

(Wheelchair user parent)

Other discussion points

Mental health service users and parents of disabled children spoke about the use of medication. There seemed to be little knowledge of the effects. Two parents said they did not give their child the prescribed medication because they were afraid of the effects. Ritalin appeared to be prescribed on an *ad hoc* basis as a means of control and users were not given the reassurance of research findings on the after-effects. However, it does seem that efforts are being made to offer social support to mental health service users in place of medication, though this was patchy and not always co-ordinated.

Physical access was a major concern. After all these years, building regulations and disability legislation, disabled people and disabled children's parents still had to consider these issues. There is only one full-time access officer in the county. Perhaps all planning applications should go before the local access groups. People felt that the physical barriers that prevented them from entering mainstream life should be addressed. Why should people have to worry about them when all they wanted to do was live the same sort of lives as other people? If schools, colleges and places of employment were accessible, disabled people could have the same education and employment opportunities as anyone else.

More control over personal care and domestic chores done by care assistants was an issue that people wanted to discuss. One older person said she had had three different assistants in the same week and now employed a local girl. A female wheelchair user said that the male partner of a woman assistant came to help her in the evenings. People needed to trust the assistants that came into their homes. Older people wanted to control the work that assistants did in their homes. National standards should be used and maintained.

Positive role-modelling received universal support when discussed. Some parents thought that disabled adults should be used as trainers to show their disabled children the methods to minimise the effects of the disability. One parent received a visit from the RNIB (Royal National Institute for the Blind) who told her about keeping the house tidy and operating to a specific systematic routine. This was impossible with a sizeable family. In the event, the child found his own levels of management of the disability that did not exclude him from family life. These special routines would have meant that the family revolved around him.

Getting around

This includes:

- mobility
- transport
- wheelchairs.

People said (in the following comments, SI denotes sensory impaired):

Two men turned up and made me test my wheelchair in a supermarket. They walked behind me, shouting instructions, in front of customers. I felt humiliated.
(Wheelchair user)

I went into hospital and they didn't even show me around the ward. Even the menus weren't Brailled. I was left to it, the other patients were more helpful.
(SI service user)

We had to wait months for an occupational therapist.
(Various people)

Accessible transport is essential to all our lives. Without it how could people get to work or attend leisure events.
(SI service user)

Discussion points

Most people who took part in the project had access to a private car, so transport issues did not present as great a problem as they would, for example, to a group of visually or learning disabled people, who relied exclusively on public transport. Nevertheless, when public transport was discussed, everyone agreed that a fully accessible and frequent public transport system was an essential element of being able to access education and employment opportunities.

Living space

This includes:

* housing
* nursing and residential homes.

People said (in the following comments, DA denotes disabled adult):

> A new residential home has just opened, but they built it to minimum standards and my friend's son couldn't get his wheelchair into the lift. He was very disappointed.
> (DA parent)

> All I want to do is live with my wife. I get no privacy, the staff are very good, but, sometimes, they don't get me up until 11.30 on a Sunday. They organise trips out but they are for the older folks.
> (Nursing home resident)

I was in a hospital for ages, I shouldn't even have been there, I wasn't ill, I should have been in a residential home, if I can't go home.

(Disabled former hospital patient)

Discussion points

Housing did not figure largely at any of the eight local meetings but two participants with experience of nursing homes had a great deal to say about their time there. Both men were young and yet spent time with people who were considerably older. Both merely wanted to live at home with their families, but circumstances had made this impossible in the short term. Both had no complaints about their treatment, but felt isolated and unfulfilled. One had to spend time in a local hospital, although he had no medical reason to be there. Agencies that should have been working together to find solutions in both instances failed to do so. Both men spoke of their human rights being infringed and, clearly, young men do not want to spend time in inappropriate places with people from different generations.

Conclusions and preferred outcomes

When the Living Options Project reached its conclusion in October 1994, service users said that emotional well-being was the area that received least attention. That project involved disabled adults receiving community care services and, therefore, had a much narrower focus but it seems that the ingredients of well-being, rights, information and advice are still absent. Having information and correct advice, and knowing rights, will enable choice and decision making, and lead to the type of independence enjoyed by the rest of society. People need to feel good about themselves and to build the confidence to take part in society as an independent and contributing member. Unfortunately for social and health care users, the support required is so scattered among different agencies and unco-ordinated that very few users manage to become independent societal members. Different agencies and different parts of the same agency appear to users to work to their own agendas. Each has its own bit of a person to take care of, relating to age, disability or emotional need. This very inflexible system obviously does not work for service users. The quotations reflect this and, to add authenticity, no attempt has been made to classify them into an order that reflects service delivery. Although jumbled in this report, they are all interlinked and significant to service users.

Outcomes

National

1   National standards of service based on equality, attitudes, language.

2   A national evaluation group of service users to ensure national standards are maintained.

3   British Sign Language to be recognised as a language and taught in all schools to all children.

4   Assessment procedure that will satisfy all agencies, but service users always in control of information destination.

5   All agencies to work to the same equal opportunities policy.

6   Published rights handbook, advising users of what to expect from service providers.

Local

1 An open and honest consultation with service users to discuss the whole area of provision.

2 A commitment to the Shaping Our Lives (SOL) model of local consultation.

3 A published structure of accountability – social services department, health authority, scrutiny panel, etc.

4 More investment in advocacy services.

5 A formal role-modelling service. Disabled children need to meet disabled adults at the earliest opportunity.

6 All social and health care staff to undergo disability equality training as part of the induction programme. Disability is as much an equality issue as black and gender issues.

7 A single information point, in the independent sector.

8 Accessible information available in all agencies.

9 Agencies to work together to challenge the societal barriers that disable people with impairments, i.e. social services, health authority, education and employment services, housing, transport.

10 Each local authority to employ a full-time access officer.

11 An independent inter-agency complaints procedure.

PART III

INFLUENCING OUR FUTURE IN SHEFFIELD
CONFERENCE REPORT

6 THE INFLUENCING OUR FUTURE CONFERENCE

Introduction

Influencing Our Future in Sheffield was a conference of service users in the city to discuss issues relating to user involvement in the services that we need in our everyday lives.

The conference was the result of discussions held between Shaping Our Lives, a national project set up by people who use a variety of services, and representatives from a local organisation and a group of service users in Sheffield. The original concept was for Influencing Our Future in Sheffield to hold a series of focus groups with a variety of local service users with the aim of looking at local and national policy issues.

This report will start in the first section by looking at the event itself, as any conference report, and give the thoughts and opinions of those who took part. It will then go beyond this in the second section to outline the process of planning and holding the event, and some of the difficulties encountered and the valuable lessons to be learned.

In an age of 'spin', where everything is painted bright and the cracks are often papered over, there remains an urgent need for people to be honest, to be open enough to look at difficult issues and to use their experiences to help shape a better world. The people who gave their time to make Influencing Our Future in Sheffield happen believe there is real value in 'telling it as it was'

– and, by doing this honestly, they hope they can help *influence* how people who use services and those who provide services work together.

The report of the event

What happened at the event

The plan for the day was as follows:

12.00 noon	Welcome people to the Centre
12.15 p.m.	Open the buffet lunch
1.00 p.m.	Introductions and performance
1.30 p.m.	Peter Campbell, Why are we here?
1.45 p.m.	Workshops
3.15 p.m.	Tea
3.45 p.m.	Where do we want to go from here?
4.30 p.m.	Close

Introductions and entertainment

As with any event of this kind, we were slightly late starting. After the buffet lunch, the main introductions were made by Peter Campbell, the compère, who then outlined the purpose of the event and its timetable.

The first part of the event was the entertainment with music and sketches – a fun way to bring to people's attention some of the themes it was hoped would come up in later discussions.

Mike Higgins, a well-known performer on the disability arts circuit, sang a number of songs and introduced the sketches that were performed between each song.

The sketches – written by members of the Steering Group – illustrated differing aspects of the user–provider of services' relationships.

- The first sketch highlighted how the 'demands' placed on disabled people who agree to be representatives on committees are often unrealistic and, as a result, fail to address the barriers that 'traditional' committee structures create. It showed how service providers make assumptions without asking for the right information.

- The second sketch raised issues about the rigid nature of service provision and how false assumptions can be made concerning who might be 'the user of services'. It showed the unreasonable processes and short deadlines that often accompany service providers' attempts to involve and consult service users.

- The third sketch was about the need for disabled people to have dignity and respect, but, most importantly, control over their own lives.

- The final sketch explored how service providers use language and meeting structures that stop people who use services from having their say in the services that they use.

The full scripts for the sketches are given later in this Appendix. The response to the songs and sketches was a positive one and they worked well together. Given the experiences of people who attended the event, it might have been more productive to have used the songs and sketches as a platform for discussion rather than break into a more 'traditional' workshop format.

After the entertainment, the compère spoke in more detail about the main aim of the event and why it was important that users had a chance to make their feelings known.

Workshops

Much of the afternoon was given over to workshop sessions, with participants dividing into four groups. This section gives an overview of the issues discussed in the workshops – the full text from the flipcharts used to record the key points made by the groups are given later in this Appendix.

The workshops covered a wide range of issues, looking at positive and negative aspects of current service provision, and how services could be improved.

Positive points made about services included:

- support to access leisure activities
- staff who are supportive
- services being tailored to individual needs
- the work of user groups.

These points reflect issues identified in other work by Shaping Our Lives and other research on what users value in relation to services. The valuing of supportive staff is particularly important as the relationship with staff can be a key issue in the delivery of positive outcomes for service users.

It follows from this that many of the problems with services identified by users at the event were connected with the direct relationship with staff. People commented that there was:

- inadequate support from staff
- staff who complain to users about their work
- negative attitudes from some staff towards service users.

Other criticisms that were made included difficulties with getting a social worker, inflexible social services transport (this was highlighted by several participants having to leave before the end of the conference because their transport had to go) and users believing that home care workers did not have enough time to give an adequate service – people quoted receiving one hour a week.

Another key criticism was a lack of involvement and communication with service users, with comments such as:

They decide what I need and don't listen to me.

There's a lack of communication – it's 'us' and 'them'.

Services should help and reflect what we want – it should be me deciding.

There was a particular point made about the importance of service users being involved. It was observed that carers are in control of many users' lives.

Shaping Our Lives' experiences with other projects shows that, when service users have the opportunity to give their views on services, they do not restrict themselves to a particular type of service. Users will always look at their lives as a whole and this means that they look across the boundaries between different services.

The Influencing Our Future in Sheffield event was no exception to this and participants pointed to a number of issues that fall beyond traditional 'social services':

- the 'benefits trap' making it difficult to get work
- inadequate benefits
- hospital waiting lists
- not enough housing, which means long waiting lists.

The workshops went on to look at how the situation could be improved. The key point seems to have been the belief that improving consultation and involvement would lead to better services. The comments included:

- there should be more user groups
- more involvement, more choice, more empowerment
- people listening to us
- willingness to try new ways of providing services
- get rid of jargon.

These points are particularly interesting given the background of difficulties experienced in developing this project and the disenchantment and dissatisfaction with current user involvement expressed by members of the Steering Group. It is clear that, despite this 'consultation fatigue', participants still see user involvement as the key to improving services. The issue is clearly that they want user involvement that leads to change.

In terms of the issues around wider services, suggestions for improvements included requests for help with getting a job and better public transport.

Plenary and conclusions

After a break for tea, everyone came back into one large group to see what people thought of the discussions and to talk about what might happen next. This session was led by the Influencing Our Future in Sheffield project worker, Bob Williams-Findlay, and Shaping Our Lives national worker, Michael Turner.

In his introduction, Bob Williams-Findlay said:

> Today was not about you talking and nothing happening about what you said. We want to use what we learnt today to influence what we can do tomorrow. We have no magic wand nor will we be making promises we cannot keep; we can promise, however, to make the people who deliver services aware of your concerns.

A list of the points from the plenary session is given at the end of this Appendix. These were the key issues and priorities.

1   *Money*: money to be made available for individuals – realistic levels of benefits for those who need them and an opportunity to work for a decent wage for others. Money to be made available for organisations – so they do not have to chase funding and can achieve their aims.

2   *Power*: the (mis)use of power maintains discrimination and inequality – there are still far too many systems that govern our lives and that we have no control over. It is time to demonstrate new and more effective ways of doing things, and to share the power.

3   *Choice*: we cannot have choice until we know what is available. Some people need support to take risks – try things out – if it does not work, this should not be judged as a failure. Disabled people are not allowed to fail.

4   *Access*: we need increased access to service providers – to promote new services (for example, direct payment schemes) and to challenge the countless old-fashioned services.

Having identified these issues, the event was closed with a promise that the Influencing Our Future in Sheffield Steering Group would look at how best it might raise these points with the City Council and other service providers.

Discussion with the Somali disabled people's group

There was some discussion at one of the sub-committee meetings about how some disabled people will not get involved in activities and consultation processes. Specific questions were raised about how certain groups of disabled people would not be in a position to access the Influencing Our Future in Sheffield event.

For example, there is a sizeable group of disabled refugees among the Somali community in Sheffield. Having met some representatives of this group of disabled people, Alden Chadwick from the Steering Group thought it was important to try and involve them in the Influencing Our Future in Sheffield project by organising a separate meeting, which would focus on their particular issues of concern.

Alden Chadwick and the project worker, with the support of an interpreter, met with eight disabled Somalis – three woman and five men from differing age groups – to discover what life was like for them in Sheffield.

At the beginning of the meeting, the group appointed a spokesperson who had already met Alden through the Council's service review of provision to physically disabled people.

It had to be clarified that our meeting was not a follow up from the last meeting he attended. We did this by outlining the work of Shaping Our Lives and the Influencing Our Future in Sheffield project. Alden also spoke about his role in the City Council. The Somalis also had an agenda that was simple and straightforward in its presentation: they wanted us to develop an understanding of the gap that exists between the Somali disabled community and service providers.

They knew that social services, health centres, disabled people's services and education, etc. were there to offer a service, but they bitterly complained about being 'cut off' and unaware of what, if anything, they were entitled to.

They said:

> We don't know who to ask for help, therefore, we feel isolated and abandoned.

It was pointed out to us that, as asylum seekers, the Somali community in Sheffield found life difficult as they came from a war-torn country, were unable to speak the language and had a very different culture. When their experiences of disability were added to all these difficulties, it soon became clear that they were not receiving the help they needed as disabled people.

To illustrate their point, they gave us some examples. Visually impaired people had no support with mobility so they found themselves trapped in their houses; a physically disabled person told of being left in the shower by a care worker; and a wheelchair user told of being unable to move around their own house because of poor access and they were also left alone over a number of days.

As a disabled black and minority ethnic community, they felt they had huge language and cultural barriers to overcome. From

65

their perspective, nothing was being provided for their community; their frustration was also fuelled by the fact that the isolation they are experiencing means they are not able to make any meaningful comparison between what they have and what other disabled people in Sheffield receive.

The spokesperson explained that he managed to gain some information because he 'found his own way' but he felt he was an exception to the rule.

The group was asked how the gap between service providers and the Somali disabled community could be bridged.

The general picture that emerged was that the total lack of communication between potential users and providers means disabled people have no real knowledge of what is available to them. This means the Somali disabled people have little direct access to service provision.

They were in favour of some disabled people being trained as advocates. The issue of the importance of both disabled men and women being trained as advocates was raised by the project worker but this was not picked up by the group.

Two key issues emerged, which are not uncommon in situations like this. First, the group spoke of the confusion that exists between service providers and the wider Somali community around what happens to the funding that is supposed to come from government. It was their view that this funding was not reaching the right people and, therefore, they would prefer the money to go directly to individuals who needed it.

Second, there was real criticism of the support – or rather the lack of it – from inside the Somali community itself. They felt key figures from within their own community were deliberately not informing them about their rights and entitlements, and, as a result, these people were acting as gatekeepers. The Somali Homecare Service was a particular target for some people who used examples to illustrate their points.

Some time was spent explaining the direct payments system to the group. Following lengthy internal discussion, the group said they would be in favour of this direct payments scheme because it would mean direct control of their finance and who they could have to give them support. Only one person at the meeting had heard of direct payments before.

Later, it emerged that there were some difficulties for a couple of Somali disabled people who had tried to use the scheme – it was thought that 'cultural barriers' had contributed to the difficulties.

It was also stated that:

Anything would be better than what we have now.

People shared a range of experiences. Only two out of eight people at the meeting had home care. One woman, with limited mobility, who had been in Sheffield for five years, said she had only once had help from Somali Homecare. Another person spoke of having an hour of support a day, which he received money to pay for.

Other people used their own experiences to illustrate previously made points. An older woman, who had lived in Sheffield for ten years, spoke about her loneliness and her growing fear because of an increased sight loss. Who, she asked, was going to look after her?

A newcomer to the city explained that he had been taken in by a local family, otherwise he would have had no support whatsoever. Somali Homecare provides him with one hour a day support, but refuses to discuss how he has been assessed. As a visually impaired person, he needs mobility training but this has never been provided. In his opinion, the Somali disabled people need outside support to gain their rights and to obtain meaningful information about service provision.

The meeting ended with another personal account of poor service delivery and an inadequate response from a service provider to a serious complaint.

While this meeting clearly revealed the plight of many Somali disabled people and showed how specific barriers prevent them from gaining access to service provision, it also demonstrated a certain commonality among *all disabled people living in Sheffield*.

Many of the comments made in the meeting were not too different from those expressed by people attending the event. Isolation, the lack of information, the role of community 'gatekeepers' and failure to make adequate assessments are common issues across the community of disabled people.

It has to be acknowledged that language and cultural issues mean specific strategies will need to be developed if the Somali disabled people are going to be supported and their needs met. This approach, however, does not prevent disabled people in Sheffield from looking at ways of breaking down the barriers between the two disabled communities and striving for common objectives.

Conclusions from the event

A great deal of hard work and effort went into the Influencing Our Future in Sheffield project. It is also fair to say that mistakes were made, the involvement of disabled people in the event was disappointing and the outcomes are not as clear as many would have liked.

Disabled people are still very much in the process of learning – learning how to take control over their own lives, how to organise and employ methods that help them build a collective identity capable of challenging their experiences of exclusion, powerlessness and inequality. The project was not just about achieving 'end results', it was also about disabled people exercising power and control, building partnerships, exploring new ways of working, seeing what worked and what did not.

The lessons we can draw from this project, the experiences shared and the information gathered must be channelled into strengthening the voice of disabled people in Sheffield.

The clear success of the event was to begin the process of bringing together different groups of service users in the city – not as good a start as might have been hoped for, but a start nonetheless. People enjoyed working together with different impairment groups and have an interest in pursuing this further.

It has also been shown – in several ways – that the networking infrastructure in the city is piecemeal and the voice of people who use services is certainly not strong enough. This certainly held back the project and limited the extent to which it could involve a full range of service users. The presence of an active and resourced user group/network or Centre for Inclusive Living in the city would certainly have strengthened the project.

The conference closed with a commitment to acting on the issues identified on the day. To do this, Shaping Our Lives had hoped to support work by the Centre for Inclusive Living that is currently being developed in Sheffield, to make contact with the full range of service user organisations in the city, and to look at how they want to approach user involvement and the potential to work together. Unfortunately, this has not yet proved possible.

Planning and organising the event

As noted in the introduction, the process of planning and holding the Influencing Our Future in Sheffield event was not entirely smooth. This section describes the process by which the event was planned and the difficulties involved, which will offer some useful lessons for Shaping Our Lives, for user groups in Sheffield and for other organisations in the user involvement field.

Background

The Our Voice in Our Future (OVIOF) project was set up by Shaping Our Lives in 1999 as a project to develop user involvement in a new programme of work being established by the Joseph Rowntree Foundation called the Future of Rights and Welfare.

The aim of the programme was to encourage the widest possible debate on the development of social policy. The aim of the OVIOF project was to initiate user involvement.

The project involved engaging service users at a national level through the publication of three booklets on the key issues under discussion (benefits, support services and mental health issues), which were followed up with a questionnaire. This national work was to be supported with specific work in two areas, one urban and one rural, and Shaping Our Lives initially approached Sheffield Disabled People's Forum to undertake the urban part of the work through a series of focus group meetings with different types of service users.

The Forum felt that it did not have the capacity to take the project forward but a meeting was subsequently arranged in the early summer of 2000 between Michael Turner from Shaping Our Lives and Jacquie Stubbs from the Forum, Christine Barton and John Mitchell from the Centre for Independent Living (CIL) and Alden Chadwick from the City Council.

It was agreed to take the project forward on the basis that Shaping Our Lives would take on a consultant to carry out the work and that there would be a local steering group to ensure local accountability. A job description was drawn up and sent to a number of consultants in the disability field. Interviews were carried out by Christine Barton, Jacquie Stubbs and Michael Turner with four consultants and Bob Williams-Findlay was offered the consultancy.

Bob Williams-Findlay started work on the project in the later part of 2000 and early 2001. It became apparent in January/February that there were problems in getting people and groups involved. There was very little interest in the project despite information being sent to a range of organisations, with follow-up calls to some.

What resulted was a 'chicken or egg' situation – we could not be clear about our aims without a steering group, but we could not get a steering group together without these aims.

It became clear that the idea of running a series of focus groups was not going to work. Some of the groups contacted by the project worker felt the idea was too vague and others, along with members of the Steering Group, believed people in Sheffield had already been bombarded with 'consultation exercises', which had produced little change.

Some members of the Steering Group also noted at this time that there might be problems about the worker not being based locally and the project being managed from a national base.

It was agreed that the original plan could not be followed through and the project worker began to look at other approaches. It was agreed that the best way forward was to hold an event for service users to discuss issues around the development of user involvement in Sheffield. It was particularly noted that users rarely have an opportunity to discuss 'How they are consulted' and this would be a focus for the event.

The review meeting of the Steering Group held after the event agreed that, with hindsight, there should have been a pause at this time for Shaping Our Lives to review the situation, to set out aims and objectives for the event, to identify the desired outcomes, to review roles and responsibilities of all concerned, and to identify the need for additional resources and workers.

Devising the purpose of the event

Planning meetings, which drew in new people including representatives from Speaking up for Action (a group of people with learning difficulties), a mental health service users' group and Voluntary Action Sheffield, were held in April and May 2001. Rachel Jackson, Sheffield City Council's Consultation Officer and Alden Chadwick, Principal Policy Officer (Disability) also attended the meetings.

> The day would be a chance for ... users to discuss real experiences and discover commonalities ... The event should take place in October 2001 and requires the project worker to drive the work forward to keep it on schedule.
> (Minutes)

A small Planning Group was set up as a sub-group of the main Steering Group with the remit to take the event forward and report back to the main group. The Planning Group met for the first time in early July 2001.

The Planning Group's job was to tell the project worker:

- who the event should be for
- what the event should do
- when it should be held
- where it should be held.

Before the Planning Group started its work, the Steering Group felt it would be useful to share its thoughts on why people did not get involved in consultation. Following a lengthy discussion, the following points were made.

- Some people feel that they don't have anything useful to say.

- They don't think that their experiences of trying to manage their direct payments are worth anything.

- They don't feel that they know very much about disability and are worried about saying anything.

- Direct payments cover only the cost of assistants to help with daily living, therefore, there is no money left to pay for the assistance required to attend meetings.

- Some people spend all their time managing their impairments and the disabling barriers they face, which means that they don't have any spare time to attend meetings.

- Some people with learning difficulties don't always have the confidence to speak up at meetings.

- Even when people did speak up, it seemed as though service providers did not listen and people got fed up when nothing happened.

- Many disabled people had learnt to expect second-class treatment and to struggle to lead ordinary lives; they thought that this was normal; they didn't expect things to change.

These points are included in the report to remind everyone of the difficulties that surround the development of 'user involvement' and, as Peter Beresford stated:

> ... issues around user involvement and empowerment aren't straightforward. They are complex, subtle and sometimes ambiguous.

Following this discussion, the Steering Group agreed that it was important to hear from people who did not usually get involved and that the Influencing Our Future in Sheffield event should perhaps be aimed at this group of people.

It should be noted that, while the group saw this as the right direction to take, the minutes show they were also aware of some of the problems that lay ahead.

At the Steering Group's review, some members suggested that an 'event approach to involvement' was not ultimately the right approach to the aims of the event. They argued that what was really needed was a long-term approach on the issue, which would have been beyond the scope of this project, and that it would have been more appropriate to work with people in their own environment, which would have been possible.

There were also comments that the project was over-ambitious. This was probably particularly true in relation to bringing in new service users, which came into the planning quite late in the day.

The practicalities of the event

Publicity and recruiting for the event

One of the key issues raised was publicity; publicising the event would be important. The time-scale involved meant that there was an inadequate amount of time for traditional advertisements and leaflets to work effectively, but a positive and upbeat article was written for a local newspaper.

Radio Sheffield was also approached on several occasions with regard to doing an interview about the event. It has to be noted that the station was not helpful with the approach and a complaint was subsequently lodged about its disrespectful treatment.

Beyond this, it was recognised as crucial at an early stage that publicity was about more than just adverts and leaflets, and that the event would work properly only if the project worker was able to contact people and talk to them in person.

This issue was not just about the project worker making contact with organisations and individuals, it was also about talking directly to them and getting their commitment to attend. The project worker devoted nine days to this type of 'outreach work'.

The project wanted the event to be for people who did not usually get involved; this meant people 'not known' by networks – a very difficult, if not impossible, group to reach. Even for those who are 'known' but opt out of consultation and involvement, the project worker needed some form of trail in order to make contact with them.

This trail could only be put in place by identifying 'go-betweens' – service providers, peer groups, organisations, etc. – who could put the worker in touch with individuals. A dual approach was adopted to identify these 'go-betweens': first, a trawl of organisations known to Sheffield City Council and, second, using contacts from the Steering Group and others involved in Influencing Our Future in Sheffield.

On this second point, there were concerns raised about the possible amount of work that this meant for members of the Steering Group. The Group had made it clear at an early stage that the amount of time they could put into the event was limited, but likewise the project worker was employed on a part-time basis that probably was not adequate for the task of recruiting people to the event, along with all the other organisational requirements, over such a short length of time.

This resulted in tension that had developed at the start of the project re-emerging, now based on what the Steering Group and the worker could realistically be expected to achieve in the short time available, along with the pressures of deadlines that accompany any type of event.

Over 160 organisations and individuals were sent letters and information about the event. In the letter, there was a request to pass the information on to individuals and an open invitation of a visit to talk about the event. Only four organisations made any direct contact and no one requested a visit.

Selected telephone calls to organisations confirmed that publicity material had been received and was being given to their members, but the offer of a visit met with a cool reception.

Visits were made to Speaking up for Action's members and a day centre for older disabled people. There was also the successful meeting with a group of Somali disabled people detailed earlier in this Appendix.

This meant that it was not possible to attract cross-impairment representation and people from minority ethnic background, despite extensive efforts. The overwhelming interest was coming from people with learning difficulties and from British white people. Part of this may be a result of the work of Speaking up for Action (SUFA), but this is unlikely to explain the whole story.

Communication with the deaf community, for example, suggested that this kind of event was not going to reach even the most active and involved deaf people – longer-term bridge building through outreach work was thought to be the only viable course of action. On another front, it was discovered only on the day of the event itself that people who were users of the mental health system also had an event on the same day.

With regard to people with physical impairments, there is no clear indication as to why they decided this event was not for them other than the broad arguments expressed elsewhere.

It was evident about a month before the event that only around 20 people would be able to attend, but this was judged to be viable, particularly as the participants included a number of the elusive people who were new to user involvement.

The programme for the day

It was suggested that the main focus of the event should be around questions relating to user involvement, for example, the 'why and how' to be engaged in a variety of consultation processes.

It was argued that the event itself needed to be:

- clear in its purpose/objective

- structured in a way that can engage people who have different experiences, starting points and possible expectations or contributions to make

- able to develop people's thinking/understanding/ involvement by leading them through an exploration of the issues and presenting them with a series of possible 'outcomes' at the end of the day.

The event also had to try and address key issues.

- What do we – as people who use services – and the people who provide services mean by 'consultation'?

- What have our experiences been?

- What are our expectations and desires?

- How do we build on 'existing good practice' and bring about change?

- What steps do we need to take?

The Planning Group advised the Steering Group that these five points needed to be developed as the 'core' purpose of the event and to be reflected in its activities, but, given the possible background of the attendees, this was an extremely ambitious task.

The Steering Group also discussed the possible programme for the event and suggested that it should be as non-intimidating as possible. It was hoped that the event could be enjoyable as well as having some practical use. After some debate, it was thought advisable not to have it too long – 12.00 noon until 4.00 p.m. seemed to be the best length.

The final programme had clear successes and failings. On the positive side, people were very enthusiastic about the role plays and Mike Higgins' songs – though the role plays had come with difficulty. The original plan was to have a theatre group performing on the day, but none had been available and this proved to be another demand on the already over-stretched Steering Committee and project worker.

The social side of the event was also highlighted – with the point being made that such social opportunities are rare and should not be undervalued.

Problems around the workshops and plenary sessions are detailed in the following section. There were also difficulties around the role of the compère/chair of the event. The Steering Group had decided it would be useful to invite someone with experience of user groups and meetings to act as the event's compère.

Steering Group members made a number of recommendations and several people were approached including Peter Campbell, chair of Survivors Speak Out (which is a group of mental health system survivors), who agreed to take on this role.

In practice, this role did not work very well. The role required of the compère had not been clearly defined, perhaps because it had been decided on only quite late during the planning. This situation was not helped by the venue failing to meet the access needs of the chair.

The workshops and plenary

There were problems with the organisation of the workshops on the day. The allocation of workshop places was to take place during registration – a list of attendees was prepared, but there were some people booked who had not given their names and this meant that the system failed because it did not consider that, without knowing the precise number of people who were attending, it was difficult to allocate people to different workshops.

The original plan was also to have no more than six people in each workshop and to allow people, as far as was possible, to be with friends or others of their choosing.

The outcome of this pre-organising of the workshops was that no one person took responsibility for setting up the workshops on the day and this led to a confused 'free-for-all'. Several people did try to sort things out, but this only increased the confusion. Eventually, the attendees were split into four workshops.

Discussions in the workshops varied greatly. People participating in the workshops came from a range of backgrounds, had varying experiences and differing access needs.

For some, it took a great deal of time and effort just to express themselves; others needed to relate to their personal experiences and agendas, and were not in a position to think about any wider picture.

The ways used to try to 'involve' disabled people in *expressing themselves* raise more questions than they provide answers. The barriers some disabled people face impact directly on the way that other service users are able to assist them in the empowerment process – their experience of inequality means sometimes the knowledge needed is not available to enable them to communicate in a meaningful way.

There are no common or shared goals in these situations and, while a set of guidelines had been drawn up by the project, they were difficult to apply in these circumstances.

These issues served to make the workshops feel over-long and focused. The plenary/feedback session suffered similarly and was too long and not accessible to all. These difficulties were compounded by difficulties with the venue that meant that the four groups met within the single main room of the event, which led to great difficulties with noise levels.

Shorter sessions with specific focuses might have helped. Smaller groups could also have helped, though there are obvious logistical problems with this approach.

Despite these problems, the workshops did enable people to use their time to put forward some clear and powerful feelings.

Scripts for the sketches

Members of the Steering Group devised a series of sketches to introduce themes of the day in a humorous and accessible way.

Respite care, version 1

A disabled service user and their partner are sitting around a table in discussion with a service provider.

On the table, there is a very large pile of papers and a glass of water. Each person also has their own papers.

Disabled person: *(Looks positive and upbeat)* I've heard that we can get some money – a grant – to help us have a rest.

Service provider: *(Suspiciously)* Yes *(pause)*, that might be possible.

Disabled person: You see, we both need a break, and Fred needs a bit of a rest from lifting me. It does cost more for us to go away – the hotel needs to have a big enough room, you know, so I can get around. And, we need someone to help me, which will give Fred a rest.

Service provider: *(Frowns and looks sincerely troubled)* Well *(pause)*, we professionals have to draw a practical distinction between what we call respite care and what you'd call 'holidays' *(waves hands in air making a sign for inverted commas). (Speaking slowly)* You see, respite care is where the carer and cared for actually have a break from each other, and 'holidays' are where the two go away together. *(Smiles)* A limited budget is available for short-term care, which of course includes respite care *(frowns)*, but no budget or grant finances are available for holiday breaks for carers and those who they care for to go away together.

Disabled person: *(Looking ironic)* If Fred were to go on holiday – where would I go?; could I go on a singles holiday on the Greek Islands?

Fred:	*(Anxiously)* But who's going to look after me? Who's going to sort out my medication?
Service provider:	*(Ignores Fred and can't seem to grasp the idea of a disabled person also being a carer)* Fred could go where he likes – maybe to his sister's in Cleethorpes – but *(cautionary nod)* remember it wouldn't be a large grant.
	We'd fit you into nice residential accommodation for a few days.
Disabled person:	*(Looks up to the gods for help)*
Service provider:	*(Beams happily and pulls out another huge pile of papers from under the table)* Now that we've sorted that one out, let's get on with the Welfare to Work Joint Implementation Plan. I'd like to have your comments on this outline by next Friday.

Respite care, version 2

A disabled service user (Claire) and her partner (Alden) are sitting around a table in discussion with a service provider (Tina).

On the table, there is an enormous pile of papers and a glass of water in front of Tina. Each person also has their own papers.

Claire:	*(Sounding positive and upbeat)* I've heard that we can get some money – a grant – to help us have a rest.

Tina:	*(Suspiciously)* Yes ... that might be possible.
Claire:	You see, we both need a break. And it does cost more for us to go away – the hotel needs to be one which is OK for Tag, and these hotels are often more expensive. And, Alden does need a rest.
Tina:	*(Frowns and looks sincerely troubled)* Well *(pause)*, we professionals have to draw a practical distinction between what we call respite care and what you'd call 'holidays' *(waves hands in air making a sign for inverted commas). (Speaking slowly)* You see, respite care is where the carer and cared for actually have a break from each other, and 'holidays' are where the two go away together.
	(Smiles) A limited budget is available for short-term care, which of course includes respite care *(frowns)*, but no budget or grant finances are available for holiday breaks for carers and those who they care for to go away together.
Claire:	If Alden were to go on holiday – where would I go? Could I go on an 18–30s holiday in the Greek Islands?
Alden:	*(Anxiously)* But who's going to look after me? Who's going to help me sort out my new medication?

Tina:	Sorry, Alden, but you're not the disabled person.
Alden:	But …
Tina:	You see, Claire, Alden could go where he likes – maybe to his sister's in Cleethorpes – but we wouldn't be paying for that. We'd fit you into an 'RNIB Rest Home for the Bewildered' for a few days.
Claire:	*(Sighs)*
Tina:	*(Beams happily and drags the enormous pile of papers across the table)* Now that we've sorted that one out, let's get on with the Welfare to Work Joint Implementation Plan. I'd like to have your comments on this brief outline by next Friday.
Claire:	Good God!

Plain language?

A group of disabled service users (Karl, Chris, Michael, David, Jason and Paul) are sitting around a table in discussion with a service provider (Alden).

Alden:	Tina has told me that you want to know more about how the Council funds organisations like SUFA.

Group: *(Members of SUFA nod or say yes)*

Alden: Good! Good! Well … I think you need to know about the SSD's [Social Services Department's] revised procedures for managing funding to the voluntary sector, which now distinguish clearly between grant aid and a contract relationship for services delivered.

Group: *(Members of SUFA begin to look puzzled, but say nothing)*

Alden: *(Reads from his notes)* On 19 March 2001, Cabinet approved payments to specific independent sector providers of care, including voluntary organisations funded both through grant aid and partnership contracts. However, Cabinet also noted that the distinction between grants and contracts was unclear and recommended that further work was undertaken on procedures and decision-making routes with respect to voluntary sector funding.

Group: *(Members listen)*

Alden: Following receipt of guidance from the City Solicitor, I can now give a clear definition, which differentiates between grant aid and contracts for services delivered.

Group: *(Members look hopeful)*

Alden:
A number of funding agreements for services currently exist with the voluntary sector by either the grant aid route or partnership contract route. This currently involves different procedures and processes for funding and administration. The choice of funding route was made historically and the rationale lost in the mists of time. The officer group charged with ensuring consistent approaches to the funding of the voluntary sector has spent some time looking at these funding routes in the light of the definitions provided by the City Solicitor.

Jason:
We don't understand!

Alden:
Don't worry, the City Solicitor passed his English exams – he can speak the language you know! Anyway ... SSD is a major funder of the voluntary sector. The Directorate has therefore worked closely with the Regeneration and Partnership Service, which is responsible for developing consistent corporate practice with respect to the management of Council funding to the voluntary sector. Officers have also been aware of the need to develop transparent and accountable funding procedures which comply with the principles set out in the local Compact between the Council and the voluntary sector. You'll remember the Compact, we consulted you about it.

Group: *(Members shake their heads)* We cannot understand what you are talking about.

Alden: Don't worry you'll get the hang of it – just be patient; you can have my notes to read.

Jason: But some of us aren't that good at reading.

Alden: Well ... this is a council procedure – it has to be written this way.

Group: *(Members frown)*

Alden: The City Solicitor has advised that contracts for services differ from grant aid in the following respects.

Group: *(Members start to look out of the window, or read papers they have brought; some look very, very sleepy)*

Alden: One. Contracts for services delivered involve the voluntary sector delivering a service commissioned by the Council and for which the Council has a statutory obligation to provide. The Council may choose to let a contract for the service to external organisations and in such cases a tender process will need to be followed in accordance with the Council's Standing Orders for Contracts.

Group: *(Members get up and leave one by one as Alden is reading from his notes – he doesn't notice and carries on)*

Alden: Two. Grant aid involves the voluntary sector delivering a service, which is one that the Council has the legal power to provide, but has no statutory duty to do so. The Council may, by way of grant aid, support the voluntary sector to provide such a service. Where the Council provides a discretionary service and the voluntary sector wish to provide a complimentary service in the same field this would also constitute grant aid. The voluntary sector may approach the Council to fund activities which they wish to undertake regardless of whether or not the Council will provide funding; the initiative therefore comes from the applicant organisation, albeit to a well advertised grant aid funding scheme.

The girls' night out

Care assistant: What are you pulling a face like that for?

Disabled person: I don't like it! What is it, anyway?

Care assistant: Come on, it's nice. It was on special offer down the supermarket ...

Disabled person: Has it got meat in it?

Care assistant: Only a bit – it won't hurt you!

Disabled person: Told you before, I don't eat meat ... it's down on my form, I don't eat meat.

Care assistant:	Think I've time to stand around reading forms all day? *(Pause)* Oh, that reminds me, I'm coming back early tonight. You don't mind do you?
Disabled person:	Well ..
Care assistant:	Staff shortages, sickness, holidays, that sort of thing.
Disabled person:	Nothing to do with the World Cup game then?
Care assistant:	I hate football. When my husband's around, I don't have much choice. He's going round a mate's house tonight ...
Disabled person:	What time?
Care assistant:	Think he said 8 o'clock.
Disabled person:	No, what time are you coming back?
Care assistant:	Oh, I don't know ... about half past six?
Disabled person:	You're joking! That's two hours early!
Care assistant:	Give you a chance to have an early night ...
Disabled person:	What if I don't want an early night?
Care assistant:	Now you're just being awkward ... Can't you co-operate; Mrs Digwall didn't mind.

Disabled person:	What time you seeing her? Bet it's about five. *(Slight pause)* Besides, Mrs Digwall's getting on a bit ...
Care assistant:	It's not as if you've got any plans, is it?
Disabled person:	How do you know?
Care assistant:	If you're doing anything, it's usually in your diary ...
Disabled person:	Hey ...
Care assistant:	Are you going to eat this or not?
Disabled person:	No, thank you. About my ..
Care assistant:	Well, if we're finished, I'd better be going or I'll be due back before I've gone.
Disabled person:	Pudding. I haven't had my pudding yet!
Care assistant:	Let's save it till later; you might enjoy it more then, eh? *(Pause)* Can I use your phone before I go?
Disabled person:	You know where it is ...
Care assistant:	*(Goes to the phone)* Hi Carol, it's Maggie. How are you? Fine. Listen, I'm calling 'cos Gary's going round Phil's. Fancy a girl's night out? Great. See you at Ginger's about half eight.
Disabled person:	Ginger's accessible, isn't it? Disabled person's toilet too, I believe ...

Care assistant:	You shouldn't have been eavesdropping …
Disabled person:	That reminds me, about my diary – could you put a new entry in before you go?
Care assistant:	Okay, but be quick …
Disabled person:	Today's date. 8.30 p.m. Ginger's. You've driven my van before haven't you?
Care assistant:	Look, wait a minute …
Disabled person:	Sorry I've not consulted you before; you know how it is, I've been too busy …

Too much – too late

Props: newspaper, post (postcard, letter, large brown envelope), diary, cereal bowl and spoon, mug and straw, waste bin.

Scene: table with the items spread over it. Waste bin is under the table. Disabled person, Christine, sitting beside the table and personal assistant, Angela, standing next to her.

Christine:	I would like to finish my coffee and then look at my diary. *(Angela offers straw and Christine takes a sip. Angela picks up the diary)*
Christine:	I'd like to look at this week please. *(Angela opens diary and holds it where she can see it)*
Christine:	It looks a bit busy. Two hospital appointments, a meeting with the Direct

Payments scheme co-ordinator, a Disability Consultative Committee meeting, a discussion about a Centre for Inclusive Living with the people from a PCT [Primary Care Trust] and a visit to Voluntary Action Sheffield. Okay, what's in today's post? *(Angela puts down the diary and moves the post nearer. She shows Christine the picture on the postcard and then turns it over)*

Christine: Cathy seems to be enjoying herself in France. I bet it's not raining there.
(Angela puts down the postcard and opens letter holding out the sheet inside for Christine to see)

Christine: Another bill, I'll see to that next week.
Angela puts the bill down and opens the large envelope. She puts a thick document on the table and holds letter for Christine to see. She reads from the letter)

Christine: I wondered when this would come. It's a draft plan about how to consult service users. Oh dear! They must be joking. Just listen to this.
(Angela is still holding letter and Christine reads from it)

'We would like you to read our revised plan, complete the questionnaire and return it to us by Friday 19 October. We are sorry about the short notice. A

	member of staff has been absent and we must finalise this plan by the end of October.'
Christine:	How can I do that in five days? How many pages are there? *(Angela turns to the back of the document)*
Angela:	60.
Christine:	And how many pages in the questionnaire? *(Angela looks at the end of the document again)*
Angela:	Ten
Christine:	It's too much, too late. Put it in the bin. *(Angela drops the document into the bin and wheels Christine away)*

Workshop flipcharts

Each workshop made a series of flipcharts highlighting the key points people were making.

Workshop A

What we use

- Day services – Home Farm Trust (timetable of activities).
- Home care services – pay directly for service.
- Residential home.
- Doctors.
- Nurses.

- Social workers.
- Occupational therapists.
- Communication therapists.
- Gateway.

What we like and dislike about the services we use
What we like:

- access to college
- walking
- art
- drama
- snooker
- sailing
- spa
- trips out
- paying directly
- some members of staff who provide the home care
- residential service open to people who are non-residents
- activities tailored to individuals via key worker
- feel safe going to see doctor who checks medication.

What we dislike:

- having an hour a week for cleaning
- complaints about too much ironing by home care workers
- transport times – own for service
- having to miss day services to go to hospital, etc.
- not enough staff to provide the service we want.

What if there wasn't a day service?

- We would be bored.
- Have to stay at home.

Comments made

Important to ask people questions about what they want.

Use key workers to have a say.

Enjoyed the day – singing, sketches, discussion about services.

Workshop B

What is it like to use services?
What we like:

- use of user groups (not enough of them!)
- more support is given
- police service
- help to get jobs.

What we dislike:

- no control over service
- may lose benefits and fall into trap
- carers have control
- attitude of drivers.

Conclusions

- Need for positive consultation.

- Need more choices – need to be more involved in running services.

- More empowerment means having more control.

What we want is

- More choice.
- More power.
- More control over homes and services.
- More user groups.

What else would you like to do to make things better?

- More communication between users and service providers.

- Need user forum.

- More money.

- Better public transport.

- Get rid of 'old-fashioned services' by trying new ways of providing services.

- People with impairments should be more in control of services.

- City Council should be more accountable – a scrutiny board.

- All types of disabled people should be represented on the Council.

- Get rid of jargon.

Comment

To be listened to and not put down …

Workshop C

What is it like to use services?

What we like:

- having own flat straight away
- staff at the hospital willing to explain things.

What we dislike:

- flats not being available – knocking them down
- had to wait a year on a waiting list
- buses and trams too crowded
- some people have bus passes – others don't
- hospital waiting lists
- staff at hospital talk to my mum, not me!
- have to wait a long time at the doctor's.

Would you like to have a say in your services?

- 'Yes, that would be a good thing ...'

How do you think you can do this?

- By joining a group like SUFA and speaking up.

Who or what would stop you?

- People don't always listen because you have a disability.
- People tell you what to do.
- Disabled people have had problems getting a social worker.

- Supported housing – community centre not being used – would like some social activities.

- Benefits are not enough.

Comments

- If you are on benefits and get a job, there could be a problem getting your benefits back if you stop working.

- 'At events like this, some people have to leave early because of transport. This means their opinions aren't heard ...'

- Benefits should be 'protected' if you try working and it doesn't work out.

- Shorten hospital waiting lists.

- More support to attend college – people can't keep up with the work because of the lack of support and equipment.

Who or what could make things better?

- John Prescott.
- Tony Blair.
- Our MP.
- David Blunkett.
- People listening to us!
- Let us have more chances to say what we think.
- Acting on what we say.
- More people joining SUFA and advocacy groups.
- More funding.

Workshop D

What we dislike about the services we use

- Transport remains inaccessible.

- Contact with social services is no good.

- They decide what I need and don't listen to me.

- A lack of communication – 'us' and 'them' – e.g. where do complaints and suggestions go?

- Services should help and reflect what we want – it should be me deciding.

They disempower us by the following:

1   Not listening.

2   Thinking they are the experts.

3   Being over-protective.

4   Being afraid of giving up their power.

5   Not collecting feedback from us – therefore:
    - not having any political influence
    - not counting the cost of dependence
    - not spending the money effectively.

Comment

1   Over the years, we have tried and failed to influence services – we want control over our choices:
    - we would like to choose what we eat
    - where we eat and with whom.

2   Ordinary choices are extraordinary for us.

3   We need new faces in planning and power.

4   New priorities.

5   More power over the providers.

Beware of disabled people – listen, don't belittle …

Points made in the plenary session

1   We want people to hear our voices and involve us in planning.

2   We need both political power and choice.

3   The failure to count the economic (and social) cost of disempowering us leaves us dependent and dissatisfied.

4   There is an urgent need for more disabled people to be in positions where they can influence and have some power.

5   We need to produce more *evidence* with regard to the negative cost of keeping us dependent.

6   Services need to be tailored to individuals' needs.

7   Identify the choices *we want* – no neat packages to fit all lifestyles.

8   Relaxing the rules (developing greater flexibility), e.g. not having a loss of benefits if someone tries working.

9 Being in a position to choose basic things:

- what you want to eat and when
- where you live
- who you live with.

10 People who never had a choice need an opportunity to learn how to be able to make *real* choices.

11 More attention needs to be paid to how we communicate – explore and cater for different methods.

12 Recognise that we don't always 'involve' people as effectively as we should.

13 Recognise the power of people coming together as one voice – being heard.

14 Exploring ways of supporting each other which are not just about meetings, administration, etc.

15 Our expertise needs to be recognised and rewarded – this could mean being paid for our contribution, time and effort.

16 There remains a problem of funding – fund raising distracts people from doing what they have come together to do.

17 Problem with short-term funding – if Council wants user involvement then it must start paying for it.

18 A key issue around consultation that needs to be addressed is what is the point of consultation without the power to influence?

19 Consultation processes are never comprehensive.

20 There is a need for consumer-centred assessments.

21 Pool, cost and analyse all the individual needs to gain evidence to improve services.

21 Centre for Inclusive Living (CIL) – Council should put long-term funding into this type of organisation rather than continue with the more traditional systems.

22 Current practice and slow movement on CIL raises doubts in service users' minds regarding Council initiatives such as Best Value.

Appendix: Notes of the planning seminar

Introductions

Everyone introduced themselves and Michael Turner gave some background to Shaping Our Lives and how the Our Voice in Our Future project came about.

Aims of the seminar

The aims of the seminar were described as being to:

- set out views on good practice in user involvement and consultation

- put together an outline for a project involving service users in developing social policy.

Initial discussion

A number of concerns were identified as being important during an initial discussion and questions:

- the need to ensure a good standard of user involvement

- the need to ensure that all voices are heard at all levels of this work, with particular concern expressed about the inclusion of people with learning difficulties

- everyone's views need to be heard and, where views are not included, this must be explained

- time is needed to consult with the organisations that people represent

- we can present all views but prioritise those of the majority

- information must be accessible

- we need to look beyond existing ideas of services to focusing on people's lives and accessing opportunities.

Consideration of good and bad practice in user involvement

This part of the seminar combined brainstorming with general discussion around user involvement.

The following were the key points to come of this.

Characteristics of good practice in user involvement

Everyone has a view worth expressing that needs to be heard.

1   User involvement must be fully accessible, and this includes addressing issues such as using accessible language, making reports and other papers accessible (i.e. Braille, tapes, accessible style for people with learning difficulties, use of minority languages, etc.).

2   There must be a distinction between user and carer involvement.

3   Involvement needs to happen in all areas – local authorities/ social services, health authorities, voluntary organisations and central government.

4   Involvement must be user led and user controlled, with service users setting the agenda(s).

5   Involvement must be based on a 'bottom-up' approach that brings in as many users as possible.

6   Involvement must be supported with accurate and sensitive information provided by an independent, user-led organisation that produces and gives out 'user-led' information.

7   User involvement must be ethnically and culturally sensitive.

8   The experience and expertise of users must be valued and respected.

9   User involvement should be part of service's 'everyday' work and decision making.

10 Involvement should aim to achieve a better quality of life for service users as citizens and we must be the ones to define 'quality'.

11 There needs to be recognition that users also contribute to society.

12 Involvement and consultation should start at a young age.

Characteristics of bad practice in user involvement

In the work of Shaping Our Lives, it has proved useful to define negative issues. This can be useful in making sure that these things do not happen and in helping us to work out the things that we do want to happen.

Negative issues identified at the seminar were as follows.

1   Token involvement without any commitment to listen and act on the views given: this particularly applies to situations where decisions have already been made and people are 'going through the motions'.

2   Stereotyping of users, which disempowers and devalues individuals and leads to our views not being heard.

3   Inaccessible involvement – including the use of inaccessible language and jargon.

4   Exclusion: this happens where there is an assumption that some users cannot be involved in making decisions. This is a particular problem for people with learning difficulties.

5   Failure to share information or communicate: this applies to communication between service providers and service users, and between different service providers.

6   Lack of understanding about the difficulties many users have in giving their views.

These positive and negative issues were identified and discussed to form a value base for the development of the project proposal.

Developing the project

The second part of the seminar focused on the shape of the project and issues related to how it should work and be organised.

We want a project that will involve users in developing a proactive agenda for social policy from a user perspective.

The project would:

- work with existing user groups to promote and inform discussion of social policy development

- address both policy and practice issues

- collate and network these discussions around user groups

- use this work as the basis for lobbying policy makers and to inform JRF's Shaping Futures programme.

We agreed that this work would best be carried out both by working with organisations of specific groups of users and by bringing together generic groups of service users.

The national organisation

This would comprise a number of workers whose role would be to:

- support user groups to carry out meetings

- provide training and guidance to ensure consistency in the work at a local level

- organise national events building on the local work

- provide and network information on policy developments to local user groups

- feed the details of the work into lobbying and political work at a national and local level.

Local user groups

Local user groups would be funded to:

- run local forum meetings to discuss and develop user perspectives on policy issues, ensuring the fullest possible participation

- use a range of methods to ensure the widest possible range of user involvement, e.g. postal surveys, internet websites and mailing list, parish magazines, teletext services, freepost leaflets and any other innovative approaches

- carry out outreach work to reach users who are not involved or who are isolated

- provide information, training and support as required for users to become involved with the project, i.e. reward involvement with new skills and knowledge.

Funding for local groups would include resources to pay all participants in the project. Some people at the seminar were concerned about saying 'nothing moves if we don't get paid' but the overall feeling was very strongly that all participants should be offered a payment, just as professionals and academics in research are paid.

Funding would also need to reflect the need to make meetings and events fully accessible in the widest sense of the word.